Knaphill

(All in One Place)

Mal Foster

Sat on the brow of what is now Woking Borough, Knaphill has emerged in stature as a village community since the mid-19th century. Its written history, however, has always been fragmented. Here you will find a crafting of a jigsaw of important historic information that the author has sympathetically brought all into one place.

Mal Foster was born in Farnham, Surrey in 1956 and brought up in nearby Camberley. His affiliation with Knaphill began in the 1970s and he eventually moved here in 1993. He is also a published poet.

Knaphill (All in one place)

Published by Publish Nation

© 2012 Mal Foster

ISBN 978-1-4717-7278-8

Cover Photograph: Lee Heather

Foreword by Cllr Melanie Whitehand

The right of Mal Foster to be identified as author of this work has been asserted in accordance with the Copyrights, Designs and Patents Act 1988

Contents

Foreword by Cllr Melanie Whitehand

Introduction

1. The Growth of Knaphill

9. Brookwood Hospital (Surrey's 2nd Asylum)

14. The Woking Invalid & Women's Prisons

20. Inkerman Barracks

23. Early Worship

29. Listed Buildings

33. Public Houses

37. War Time 1939-1945

43. Crimes and Misdemeanours

52. Knaphill and the War of the Worlds

53. Knaphill Football Club

54. The Village Identity and its Future

Acknowledgements

My very special thanks to all who have assisted me through my research, the editing process and compilation of this book: Karolyne Foster, Lesley Bowdidge, Peter Mullard, Brian Jones, John Gray, Claire Hawkins, Cllr Melanie Whitehand and Rohona Elstone at The Surrey History Centre.

I am also indebted to those who have provided a number of photographs for use in this publication: Lee Heather (Cover photo), Steve West, Brian Quaintmere, and the photographers of all the other original photographs (sadly no longer with us) who had the foresight to record such wonderful pieces of Knaphill's history.

References: The History of Woking by Dr Alan Crosby, Heritage Walks by Iain Wakeford. Memory Lane articles by Eileen Martin, Life and Work on Surrey Heath by Mary Ann Bennett, The Woking History Journal 1989-1991 edited by Iain Wakeford, Surrey Asylum (Brookwood Hospital) Annual Reports (various dates), Surrey Federation of Women's Institutes, Curators at Knaphill's various churches and their webmasters, History of Special Investigation Branch by Pat Colson, From Pub to Pulpit by Wilfred Woolvett, Living Well Centenary Magazine, Woking Prison Blogspot by Corrine Garstang, The Knaphill Azalea by Don Hyatt, The Observer, The Surrey Advertiser, Surrey County Council, Open University - International Centre for the History of Crime, Policing and Justice, Woking Borough Council, and Surrey History Centre.

I would also like to thank all those 'anonymous' internet authors whose work, in part, I have also been able to collate and digest whilst carrying out my research.

W.Johnson Greengrocers shop in the High Street c.1935

Foreword by Cllr Melanie Whitehand

Knaphill has had much to be proud of through its long history of providing service for the community, particularly through the Invalid & Women's Prisons and later the army barracks or the much respected, but now sadly defunct, Brookwood Hospital.

Unfortunately, change is inevitable, but it is how such changes are managed that will enhance or detract from what is beneficial now to local residents.

There is no doubt that in recent years, Knaphill has experienced a large explosion of development within its boundaries, more than any other ward in the borough. This has been coupled with the loss of many of the old independent trading stores which has altered the outlook on the High Street almost completely.

In going forward, I hope that this book will give its readers much enjoyment and be a lasting reminder that Knaphill is a great village blessed with a unique unerring spirit full of people who really do care for its future.

Melanie Whitehand, June 2012

Introduction

You can't rewrite history, but you can verify it and then bring it all into one place. Researching material for this book over the last few years has been a very rewarding experience. It has also become something that has bordered on an extreme, if not a mad, obsession.

Much of the history of Knaphill already appears under the umbrella of Woking. Other bits are recorded elsewhere in places such as church records, history journals and of course the local press of its day. The Surrey History Centre has also been an important source for verifying much of the data here.

National Census records and military and government archives also provide good cross-references for most of the information already at hand, particularly when researching the history of the old Brookwood Hospital and the Woking prisons that later became Inkerman Barracks.

Unfortunately, many old Woking Council records had been destroyed, meaning that some history will be lost forever.

Having attended various functions and meetings in Knaphill across the years, I have also been able to gain a unique insight from the personal recollections of those who say that they are born and bred in the village and have lived here all of their lives. There has always been an embodiment of pride and nostalgia coming from these conversations.

Knaphill is certainly rich in its own history; it also has a great underlying spirit. You just have to dig a bit deep to find it.

The Growth of Knaphill

The village name of Knaphill was derived from 'la Cnappe', with its earliest reference dating back to 1225. 'Cnappe' or 'Knap' actually means 'at the top of the hill'. The hill part of the name came about during the 15th century and is believed to be a corruption of the old English term of 'haga' meaning an enclosure which dates back to Anglo Saxon times. 'Knaphill' has previously been spelt in various ways, sometimes without the 'K' as 'Naphill' and also as 'Knap Hill.'

The village emerged as part of the ancient parish of Horsell. Horsell formed part of the Manor of Pyrford, which may explain why Horsell is not recorded in the Doomsday Book of 1086. This also means that Knaphill, along with the rest of Horsell, was probably part of the land granted to Westminster Abbey in 956 A.D.

Horsell was the property of the Abbot of Westminster by 1278 but would have passed to Henry VIII when he dissolved the monasteries in the 1530s. There is also some evidence to suggest that Knaphill and Horsell once formed part of Windsor Great Park.

The property, including what is now Knaphill, was owned by Denzil Onslow in 1678 and it continued to be held by the Onslow family into the mid-19th century when it was sold to the London Necropolis and National Mausoleum Company.

The Basingstoke Canal was constructed to the south of Knaphill and opened in 1794 and the London & South

Western Railway Company came in 1838, the nearest station being built at nearby Brookwood. Knaphill developed slowly, but not initially as a commuter village as most people found work locally. An invalid and woman's prison was established here in 1859, which was later converted into army barracks.

In the mid-19th century the London Necropolis and National Mausoleum Company owned much of the land that is now Knaphill. The heathland to the south of the village became ear-marked for the locations of what was to become the Surrey Lunatic Asylum and Woking Prisons in Knaphill as the company negotiated the sale of much of its land.

The sprawling Knaphill Common had sat snugly between Horsell and Pirbright Commons and Sheets Heath. In the 1880s neighbouring Brookwood was able to develop as a village in its own right as the railway station slowly became an important hub for the area's growing population.

At the time, the area was treated as low class and inferior. Other pieces of the land were sold off in 'quick sales' and a number of small holdings began to appear.

Dwellings were poorly built with little planning as they popped up in a somewhat sporadic fashion. By the 1870s and 1880s the remaining areas of the common had been sold for further housing and many of these became inhabited by Knaphill's so-called working class, including those employed at the prisons and the lunatic asylum.

The fertile soils in and around Knaphill proved ideal for the establishment of garden nurseries and these employed large numbers of manual workers. The earliest nursery was founded by John Waterer in the 1760s. In 1809 the nursery started to specialise in rhododendrons and this was where the famous Knaphill strain of azalea was born. The business continued to be owned by the Waterer family until 1976.

Michael Waterer (1770-1842) produced the *Nobleanum* azalea which flowers at Christmas. In 1870 Anthony Waterer (1822-1896) began hybridising using the species and developed hybrids of the deciduous rhododendrons that included hybrids from Belgium and others from eastern North America, China, and Asia. Then in the 1920s they were hybridised even further by Lionel Rothschild of Exbury Gardens in Hampshire. The Knaphill azalea features on the Woking Borough Council village emblem for Knaphill. Knaphill Football Club has replaced the azalea with a football for their club badge.

Knaphill Brickfields, which was located just off Anchor Hill, had been a key employer in the village since the early 1760s. Bricks from the site were used for the construction of the Basingstoke Canal, Surrey County Asylum and Knaphill's two convict prisons. The works were owned and operated by the Cook brothers and were situated where the Lansbury Business Park is today. It was accessible from Lower Guildford Road and had an entrance at what is now Hillside Close off Anchor Hill. The distinct 'yellow' bricks from the fields were also used to build a number of residential dwellings in and around the village. The business was closed down in 1924-25 because of depleted sand-clay levels and the numerous alternative options that became available in the construction industry around that time, although some 'red' bricks were still produced from the pits adjacent to Robin Hood Road and in St John's right up to 1942.

Nearly all of Knaphill's residents near the end of the 19th century were new settlers who had come from all over the British Isles and many returning from spells overseas. Out of a total of 52 people, who were mostly children, were said to be born in Knaphill, only one family, that of John Cheeseman, a nursery worker aged 47, could claim to be 'Knaphill born and bred,' while over 50 people given as born in Knaphill, mostly older, had moved away from the village around that time.

According to an advertisement in a copy of the *Reading Mercury* dated 3 November 1873, the village of Knaphill held a regular cattle market and livestock fair. These dated back at least 200 years and rivalled a similar fair (or fayre) in Blackwater near Camberley which ran until the 1920s.

It is not clear where the site of the 'Knaphill Fair' actually was, but further investigation shows that there are a number of references to Bisley, which suggests that the fair took place on or near the Knaphill/Bisley border, perhaps on the edge of Knaphill Common at Limecroft Road. Rather interestingly, cattle are now regularly grazed near the site at Stafford Lake as part of a Surrey Wildlife Trust project to protect and restore natural habitat.

A rare photograph of a Knaphill School class taken in the early 1900s

Knaphill's first school, which was situated in the High Street, opened in the early 1860s and by 1881 had expanded to accommodate up to 200 local children. The school was expanded further in 1884 and again in 1906 with enough places available for 450 children. The school was originally run by the Woking School Board from March 1877 before transferring to Surrey County Council in 1903.

At the beginning of the 20th century Knaphill was a small hamlet of just a few houses and farms clustered at the foot of Anchor Hill. At the top of the hill was the Anchor Hotel with its stables and a small thatched farmhouse. Apart from a few houses that were starting to emerge along the Broadway and what is now Chobham Road, there was nothing except common land between the village centre and Brookwood Station. Various tracks and paths led across what remained of

Knaphill Common. In summer these tracks were very sandy, but in winter they became extremely muddy. It was an ancient practice to cut gorse, heather and shrubbery from the common to lay upon the tracks to make them suitable for horse traffic.

Squatters, usually gypsies, would pitch little wooden shacks on part of the common land. If they remained there for a long time without attracting any attention, then they would attempt to legally claim the land from the authorities. By 1905 a number of brand new terraced and semi-detached cottages were selling for an average price of £450. The very same properties now command a selling price of around £300,000.

By the 1920s Knaphill was a detached rural village surrounded by rolling lush countryside, woodland and important heathland. There were still fewer houses in Knaphill itself but it could boast a vibrant village centre that attracted many people from the surrounding areas.

One of four local butchers in the village was Grimditch & Webb in the High Street. They owned two slaughterhouses, which meant that cattle, sheep and pigs were a common site as they were herded through the village to meet their fate. To the rear of the High Street was Highclere Farm. Part of the farmhouse still stands today and is currently occupied by Pets Kingdom in the High Street. The farm consisted of stables, cowsheds and agricultural land where it joined with Blue Gates Field at Waterers Nursery (now Waterers Park).

The Co-operative Society owned the small iconic building at the junction of High Street and Broadway where Mann's estate agents are now situated. The single-storey shop was built around 1905. Other retailers were Mingays the fruiters, which also sold fresh fish and vegetables; International Stores; Wilsons; and Ruglys the draper's store, which later became Boormans, the jewellery shop.

Another slaughterhouse in the village centre was Moore's, with livestock pens and a huge yard to the rear. One of the busy village bakers was the Embledon Bakery across the High Street from the Anchor Hotel. Another was Pickards, also in the High Street further up towards The Crown Inn. Opposite the Crown stood W.Johnson the greengrocer and fruitier shop, which later became Knaphill Butchers. The building still stands today and is now occupied by a takeaway kebab shop. A large furniture store was situated in Anchor Hill and stood at its junction with Barley Mow Lane.

There were also a number of confectioners in the village and the Post Office was called Belchers at the time. Belchers stood between the High Street and Fosters Lane near to where the Total petrol station is situated today. The Post Office contained a telegraph room where telegrams could be sent and a mail sorting office was situated at the side. The village ironmonger was F.G. Rice who sold a huge range of tools and gardening ware, as well as fixings and fastenings, all sold by weight. China and glassware was sold upstairs and there was a coal yard to the rear.

The cycle repair shop was Trotters, who also recharged the large crystal batteries that were popular at the time, and the cobblers and shoe shop was run by a Mr Hill. The Forcett family owned the village rag-and-bone yard.

Some houses had small 'shops' in their front rooms and many gardens in the village had plots for vegetables and orchards, while beehives were common in the open spaces between the cottages. Of course it was all so very different from how the village looks now.

Junction at Lower Guildford Road and Barrack Road (now Victoria Road)

Brookwood Hospital (Surrey's 2nd Asylum)

One of the major employers in and around Knaphill until its closure in the mid-1990s was Brookwood Hospital, described as a vast, purpose-built lunatic asylum that dated from the late Victorian era and was constructed on Knaphill Common. The hospital, designed by architect Charles Henry Howell, started life as The Surrey Asylum and formed part of the southern boundary of Knaphill that is denoted by the section of the Basingstoke Canal between Bagshot Road and Hermitage Road adjacent to Brookwood Lye.

The lunatic asylum was established in 1867 by Surrey Quarter Sessions as the second County Asylum (the first being Springfield Asylum in Tooting) and from then until its closure in 1994 it served as the leading mental hospital for the western half of the county.

During World War II, it also served as an emergency war hospital. The surviving records which are held by Surrey County Council are extremely abundant and provide a very full and rich picture of the government and administration of the hospital and of the medical care provided. They also reflect the functioning of this vast institution as a self-contained community with workshops providing practical and therapeutic training, a farm providing food, for internal consumption and sale, and a constantly changing programme of entertainments.

According to reports submitted by Surrey County Council's 'Lunatic Asylum Visiting Committee' on 9 November 1897, there were serious concerns over health and safety at the establishment.

The gas works had been enlarged and improved and a better cooking apparatus had been provided. However, continuing problems with drainage and sewage needed to be dealt with urgently. The water supply had been receiving urgent attention and the deep well still had to be constantly tested with regard to its yielding capacity. This was a major problem at the hospital and rainwater had to be utilised for washing laundry. In 1897 four cases of Typhoid Fever had been diagnosed among the patients. Surrey County Council went to great lengths to contain the outbreak and prevent reports of it being leaked to the local community and the press.

Although this was a serious problem, the general treatment and management of the patients was found to be 'careful and considerate' and carried out in a 'humane manner'. Despite the hospital's obvious teething problems and the Typhoid outbreak, Samuel Brooks, chairman of the visiting committee, deemed that the asylum and all its departments were being run efficiently.

In November 1899 there were a total of 1,106 patients on the wards, which led to serious over-crowding; in fact, the very problem that resulted in this 2nd asylum being created in the first place. A request was made for additional wards and these were eventually added during 1903-04.

A 1904 audit shows that patient numbers had increased to 1,296. The weekly maintenance charge for each patient was twelve shillings (60p). There were also concerns over staff turnover as less than 50% of nurses stayed to complete over one year of service. The hospital had a very high mortality rate and the audit shows that with 188 new patients admitted, 79 patients had died (47 being women) and just 62 had been discharged following their recovery from illness.

There were also reports of fires on the wards and patients gaining injuries such as fractures from the actions of other patients. *Colitis, erysipelas,* and *influenza* were rife throughout the hospital. Further outbreaks of Typhoid had also been recorded. Some patients also died from bedsores.

As bed fires were just one of a number of fire related problems, the hospital had its own dedicated part-time fire brigade. One of its fire chiefs between 1974 and 1977 was Harry Sale, who lived with his wife and children in the tied cottage, North Lodge, which was located where The Vyne community centre and doctor's surgery stand today. Mr Sale, who had retired to Oxfordshire, sadly passed away in 2011.

The hospital played a key role in the development of Knaphill. It was a major employer in the area for doctors, nurses, and ancillary staff, as well as maintenance and support workers.

In the hospital grounds was a farm that boasted cows, sheep and a small piggery that was situated just about where The Vyne car park is now. Shire horses also grazed on the farm. Old photographs of the site show that the hospital driveways were lined with rows of impeccably kept rhododendron bushes that were constantly maintained by the patients. A cinema which sometimes opened for use by local residents was a major source of recreation at the hospital.

Each August Bank Holiday the hospital held a large village fete on its main playing field where local people could purchase produce direct from the farm. They could also buy handicrafts made by the patients in the workshops. Many hospital staff lived in designated hospital cottages in Oak Tree Road Spur and in Sparvell Road.

The Surrey Lunatic Asylum's name was changed to Brookwood Hospital in 1919 to make it easier for patients and visitors travelling by rail to Brookwood Station to locate.

The hospital was run by the Surrey County authorities until 1948. It then came under the National Health Service as the West Surrey and North East Hampshire Health Authority until its eventual closure in 1994.

Most of the hospital grounds have now been redeveloped, the wards having made way for the Sainsbury's and Homebase superstores and a large number of houses and apartments. The central building, Florence House, which is Grade II listed, has been retained and converted into luxury flats. Several of the new residential roads were named after the old hospital wards or prominent hospital staff.

The former Brookwood Hospital chapel situated in Brushfield Way is now a Buddhist Monastery housing *The Dhammakaya International Society of the United Kingdom* and its former mortuary is now living quarters to the monks. The old water tower, which formed an integral part of the Knaphill skyline, did not survive the redevelopment of the site, although the clock tower at Florence House remains and is still synonymous with Knaphill's unique identity as we know it today.

It's interesting to note that the emergence of the asylum and that of the Woking prisons both built on land purchased from the London Necropolis and Mausoleum Company should lead to the devaluation of other properties in Knaphill, though.

Knaphill had often been described as a convenient 'dumping ground' for those decision makers in local government and just about far enough away from central Woking to readily accommodate some of the country's most notorious criminals, as well as some of its most insane.

Gasworks Cottages at The Surrey Asylum, Knaphill c.1881

The Woking Invalid & Women's Prisons

In the mid-19th century the Home Office purchased around 65 acres of land in Knaphill from the London Necropolis Company to build a special prison for disabled (mental/physical) convicts. It was designated 'The Woking Convict Prison' and was to be the first of its kind. Construction of the site began in 1859. It received its first officers and inmates a year later when they were transferred from Lewes, Carisbrooke, and Dartmoor prisons. These male convicts helped construct it to reduce costs. In 1869, one hundred females were transferred from Parkhurst on the Isle of Wight and employed on laundry, cooking, tailoring, and other duties. By 1870 its population had grown to an average of 610 and included both male and female miscreants. An additional twenty acres of adjacent land was purchased and building was ongoing until 1892. The disabled wing was given over to the army in 1895 and converted to quarters for infantry troops. The female wing continued to be used until 1895 when, like all the male prisoners who had been transferred to other prisons earlier, the women were sent to Holloway in London.

Many of the inmates at the Knaphill Women's Prison were convicted of murdering their own children. Some were originally sentenced to death, but then had their sentences commuted to life imprisonment.

One was Mary Hannah Leach, who was born around 1864 in Westfield, near Guiting Power. Mary Hannah was spotted walking along a canal towpath towards Cirencester with her daughter Minnie in her arms. There was no sign of her son,

Henry, who was fathered by Thomas Townsend. After a short search, the body of little Henry was found floating in the canal. At the subsequent trial Mary Hannah was found guilty of murder and sentenced to death. However, she was then found to be pregnant again with another of Thomas Townsend's children and her sentence was reduced to a prison term. In the late spring of 1886, Reuben George Leach was born. Mary Hannah was then sent to Knaphill Prison, where her name appears on the 1891 census.

Another unfortunate soul was Frances Isabella Stallard who was born in Chale in 1856. In 1875 she gave birth to an illegitimate daughter. In 1877 she was found guilty of murdering the child. Her death sentence was later commuted to life imprisonment and she was sent to serve her time at Knaphill. After being transferred to Holloway she was later released from prison and is known to have died at Brading on the Isle of Wight in 1922.

Lucy Lowe was born in Stagsden in Bedfordshire as Lucy Riddy in 1841 and was one of twelve children. She gave birth to a child in January 1876, whom she then murdered in March the same year before returning to her employment in Hampstead. She was sentenced to be hanged but was shown clemency after she confided her remorse to a chaplain whilst awaiting her fate in Bedford. Lucy was then moved to Knaphill Prison where she appeared in the 1881 census. She was then 39 years old.

One of the most famous inmates at the prison was perhaps Mary Prout, who is the subject of a song by Tom Bliss. His haunting song *'The Sin of Mary Prout'* is included on his album The Whisper. Mary Prout had killed her young baby Rhoda in 1863 following a bout of post natal depression. Mary was sentenced to twenty years imprisonment, although this was reduced to ten years, of which most was served in Knaphill Prison.

Susannah Hyde, the wife of a shoemaker from Oxfordshire, killed one of her children, a boy of about three years of age, by nearly severing his head from his body with a razor, and afterwards tried to kill herself, first by attempting to cut her own throat and then by trying to strangle herself with some pieces of twine. The woman had previously shut another child, a girl a little older than the deceased, in the next room. The girl witnessed her brother's murder and her mother's attempted suicide through a crack in the door. A verdict of wilful murder against Susannah Hyde was returned. Her trial took place on 2 March 1870 in Oxfordshire, where she was tried for murder and sentenced to hang. After a spell at Millbank Prison, she was transferred to Knaphill and appeared in the 1881 census. The death sentence was never carried out.

In 1875 Rosina Rue from Pitney, Somerset confessed to the murder of two young children, as well as the arson of her then master's property. The case was widely reported at the time and made the national newspapers. She was tried and found guilty of manslaughter. In March 1876 she was given a life sentence at Taunton. She died aged 25 years old whilst at Knaphill Prison on 8 December 1884 from a kidney inflammation, and was buried in a pauper's grave four days later at Brookwood Cemetery.

Not all the convicts were child murderers, though, and one of the prison's most infamous incumbents was Rachel Leverson, or Madam Rachel Leverson, as she preferred to call herself.

In the legal section of *The Graphic* dated Saturday, 23 October 1880, the following was reported: *Madame Rachel, the person who became notorious a few years ago as claiming the power to make people "beautiful for ever" and who, after suffering seven years penal servitude for fraud, was convicted a second time in 1878, died in Woking Prison, Knaphill last week from dropsy. An inquest was heard and the jury returned a verdict of "Died by the Visitation of God".*

Madame Rachel (aka Sarah Rachel Leverson or Levison and Sarah Russell) was a British criminal and con-artist in Victorian-era London during the late 19th century. Operating a prominent beauty salon, from which she personally guaranteed her clientele everlasting youth (using grandiose-sounding concoctions comprising of everyday ingredients such as bran and water), she would blackmail many wives of London's so-called upper class.

The female prison was also 'home' to the infamous Florence Maybrick, who was convicted of poisoning her husband, James Maybrick, with arsenic in Liverpool in 1889. Over 100 people lined the streets of the village when she was transferred here in August that year. Nowadays, it is her husband who attracts the most interest as one of the main Jack the Ripper suspects.

On her journey into Knaphill Prison, Florence Maybrick famously wrote..... *"We drove through lovely woods, the scent of flowers was wafted by the breeze into what seemed to be a hearse that was bearing me on toward my living tomb"*.....

During the 1870s, Dr William Orange, a senior doctor at Broadmoor in Berkshire, recommended that many of their patients would be best accommodated at the Woking Invalid Prison at Knaphill, as their personal status had declined due to ill-health.

The names of those transferred do not exist in any known public record but one Thomas Dixon is a perfect example of the type of person that ended up in Knaphill. In 1861 he was charged with attempting to murder his wife at Parr, Lancashire. He was found guilty and sentenced to penal servitude for life. Thomas Dixon, who was a watchmaker by trade, ultimately died at the prison.

Another infamous inmate was the Irish Republican leader Charles J. Kickham, who was born on 9 May 1828. Kickham joined the Irish Republican Brotherhood (IRB) or the Fenians in 1860. On 15 September 1865 the Dublin Police took possession of the *Irish People* headquarters at 12 Parliament Street and seized the entire contents of the office. The few members of the staff still on the premises were arrested and others were picked up on the street or in their homes. The *Irish People* documents revealed Kickham's role in the Fenian conspiracy. On 11 November 1865 he was arrested. Nearly blind and almost completely deaf, Kickham was charged for writing 'treasonous' articles and for committing high treason. He was tried before Judge William Keogh and sentenced to fourteen years penal servitude. He was sent to Mountjoy Prison. On 10 February 1865 he was transferred to

Pentonville Prison near London. During this time his health deteriorated and this was blamed on a poor prison diet. On 14 May 1866 he was transferred to Portland Prison and later to Knaphill where he spent the remainder of his term. He was released in 1869 with his health severely impaired and returned to Mullinahone, Co. Tipperary.

Two American brothers, who swindled the Bank of England in Threadneedle Street in London, were also incarcerated at the Invalid Prison. In 1873, George and Austin Bidwell stole an incredible £500,000 from the bank. They achieved this by simply writing false cheques in the name of Horton & Co and convinced the institution that they were running a reputable business. Their story was highlighted in the *New York Times* of 1892 as their sister fought tirelessly for their release.

In 1877, Harriet Staunton's husband, Patrick, and three others were accused of starving her to death at Penge and lurid newspaper reports of the 'Penge Murder Mystery' trial as it became known held the nation's rapt attention. Patrick Staunton died of consumption in Knaphill Invalid Prison in 1881 at the age of 28. A bestselling novel about the murder, written in 1934 by Elizabeth Jenkins, has recently been republished.

Inkerman Barracks

Royal Military Police passing out parade, Inkerman Barracks, February 1953

Inkerman Barracks was so-named after a battle in a place of the same name in the Crimea, Russia in 1854. Now it housed the 2nd Battalion Royal West Surrey Regiment, also known as 'The Queen's Regiment'.

The former prison's conversion to a barracks was completed in 1903, when the 1st Battalion Royal Berkshire Regiment moved in. They were replaced by the 1st Battalion Royal Scottish Regiment from 1904 to 1905, followed by the 2nd Battalion Royal West Sussex Regiment (1912 to 1914). The barracks were then used as a military hospital during World War I and then remained vacant until the 1st Battalion Royal Warwickshire Regiment moved in from 1925 to 1927.

The 2nd Battalion Royal Warwickshire Regiment occupied the barracks from 1930 until 1935. They handed over to the 1st Battalion Royal Welsh Fusiliers, who left Inkerman in 1937. During World War II, a cinema (later called The Globe), some wooden 'Spider' huts, and other temporary structures like the gym, were added at the rear of the main buildings.

In the spring of 1947, when the Military Police Training School moved from Mychett, it was decided to include an Special Investigation Branch (SIB) training school, and the first course of 10 men completed their six weeks of training just before Christmas 1947. The Military Police gained their 'Royal' title in September the same year.

The training school was situated in a building at the side of the Officer's Mess, just outside the main barracks, and its students were accommodated in the four rooms on the first floor. As Inkerman Barracks had previously been a prison, there were still wrought iron bars fixed across some windows which added to its foreboding and gloomy appearance. Needless to say, the ablutions there were very basic.

All the SIB students wore civilian clothes and were all ex-civilian policemen or had been recruited from British Army units cross the globe, and at the end of the course, some of the senior Non Commissioned Officers were promoted to Lieutenants and went on to later become Deputy Assistant Provost Marshalls within the SIB.

For all recruits, apart from the parade ground and assault course, the barracks had classrooms for basic learning such as map reading, how to handle prisoners, Corps history, discipline, the army organisation and its acts, powers of arrest, judge's rules, court martials, factual report writing, road traffic accidents, investigation techniques of probe and search, physical training in the gym, and unarmed combat. All of this with a view to each new soldier gaining proficiency points.

The regiment's sleeping quarters were sombre with walls painted a very drab green with 30 young men to a room. Each man had a small wooden locker plus a wooden bed box placed at the foot of the bed. Kit was arranged in typical military fashion and inspections were frequent.

In 1965, local opposition to the demolition of this historic site was ignored by the then Woking Urban District Council and the bulldozers and wrecking ball were sent in to do their worst. It had been hoped that the iconic clock tower and arch might be saved as it was a local landmark, but, unfortunately, it wasn't to be.

The whole site was eventually sold to the Woking Urban District Council and The Guinness Trust, who began developing it as a housing estate in the early 1970s. Building continued until the 1990s. All that remains of the original buildings is the prison officers' quarters on Wellington Terrace and Raglan Road. These were fully restored and sold for occupation. Queens Road and Sussex Road (both in Knaphill) are named after two regiments that were based at Inkerman Barracks.

Early Worship

The Holy Trinity Church was built here in 1885. Known affectionately as 'the old tin church' it was a corrugated iron structure lit by oil lamps and heated by two large round iron stoves. Because Knaphill was so small, the church didn't have a parish of its own and was part of the St John's parish and remained so until 1967. In 1896 a small church room was built, which later became the end of the Hall, roughly where the stage and cloakrooms are now. However, the church community had a much more ambitious vision. Plans for a new, more substantial building had been drawn up in 1893 by the architect, J. Henry Ball. The original plans included a spire, although this was never added during construction.

The foundation stone was laid on 23 March 1907 by H.R.H. Helen, the Duchess of Albany, wife of Queen Victoria's youngest son. Apparently, there was much excitement as the Duchess was driven in a carriage from Woking railway station to Knaphill. Members of Woking Fire Brigade formed an arch across Goldsworth Road and triumphal arches had been placed at the entrance to Goldsworth Road, Kiln Bridge, and Knaphill High Street. The foundation stone was laid in the low wall at the chancel steps where it can be seen today inscribed, *'a symbol of Christ who alone is the foundation of all our life and of all our worship'*.

On the back of the wall you can see names carved by some of the bricklayers, who used the less common red bricks from the Knaphill Brickworks. If you look closely you'll see that there are different bricks in the west wall facing the road. This is because of changes in the original plans which saved

£1,200. Out of the old building came the wooden pulpit, reading desk, and font. The bell was relocated on the front wall of the new church where it is still occasionally used. The alabaster font now in the church was presented by the Wigan family, and finally, the new building was consecrated on 25 September 1907. There was still work to do on the building, however. In 1915 a £300 organ was installed and in 1923 the pulpit, designed of alabaster to match the font, was dedicated as a memorial to the fallen of the 1914-18 Great War.

An early view from inside Knaphill's Holy Trinity Church in Chobham Road

During World War II there was little change, except that the church was licensed for the solemnisation of marriages on 30 December 1941. Up until that date all weddings had taken place at St. John's, the then Knaphill parish church.

In July 1948, the 1939-1945 Roll of Honour plaque was dedicated to the men and one woman of the village who had perished. It can be found on the low wall to the right of the World War I memorial pulpit.

***

Early members of the Knaphill Methodist Church held open air services on Anchor Hill from 1865, partly in an attempt to dissuade people from playing cricket there on a Sunday. Help in conducting these services was given by local preachers from Guildford. Soon Wesleyan Ministers formed a Sunday school which met first in a barn and then in The Royal Oak public house at the foot of Anchor Hill.

The membership of the new Methodist Society grew and a chapel was erected at the top of the hill and opened in 1867. It prospered and ten years later a hall was built for the use of the Sunday school.

During the 1870s the chapel remained evangelical. By the early 1880s there were several qualified local preachers in the village. The 25th anniversary of the Sunday school was celebrated in 1890 and in 1897 a Wesley Guild was formed.

In 1912 the Trustees realised that improvements to the chapel were necessary and fund raising efforts began. The renovations were completed by 1917 and a formal re-opening was held.

After the war the chapel continued to thrive. In 1924 a Sunshine League for young people was formed and in 1926 a Primary Department to the Sunday school was started. It soon became obvious that an extension was needed in order to cope with all the chapel activities. However, building work had scarcely begun when it was discovered that the original Hall was unsafe and a completely new school would have to be built. This was opened in 1928.

During 1935 the church itself was found to be beyond repair. One of the Trustees, Frank Derry, made a generous offer to finance a new church and this was opened in November 1935.

***

The founder of Knaphill's Baptist Church was Robert Lloyd, who came to Knaphill with his wife and four young children in June 1867. Robert Lloyd came from Rugby, Warwickshire, to be head gardener at the newly opened Surrey County Asylum. He was responsible for the laying out of the grounds and gardens and planned many of the building developments. He later became well known as a local horticulturist and landscape gardener and was consulted on the layout of the grounds of other hospitals in the region.

Robert Lloyd was a committed Christian, a member of the Churches of Christ, and had a passion to share his own living faith with others.

In 1882 Hope Chapel, as the new building in the High Street was called, was something of a landmark in the village. The solid brick construction of the church was described at the time as 'the most modern building in Knaphill'.

It is believed that the land was given by John Potts, one of the founder members, who was also Governor of the women's prison in Knaphill around that time.

The cost of the building, which included the present sanctuary, the vestry, and a small lean-to at the back with earth closets, a store and sink, was £370. The church was helped by a loan from Robert Black, in whose Chelsea home the first converts had been baptised. A successful businessman, he encouraged the founding of Churches of Christ congregations in the London area and had helped the Knaphill 'venture' from the start.

In 1892, membership of the church stood at 78. In January of the same year, the building was registered for marriages, and the first wedding, that of Miss E. T. Lloyd and Mr. F. W. Halsey, took place on the following 30 June.

In December 1911 members of the church, along with auxiliary workers from the nearby Lunatic Asylum, helped form the Knaphill Working Men's Club in Highclere Road.

Another Baptist Church is the Providence Baptist Church in Robin Hood Road, Knaphill. The site has been that of a Baptist church in various forms for over 140 years, however, the present church was only officially formed in 1933. The building has undergone various changes through its history and in 1998 the old side room was demolished and replaced by a larger multi-purpose area, which is now used for worship and many other activities.

***

The earliest records of the St Hugh of Lincoln Catholic Church in Knaphill is that of a 13th century hermitage owned by the Dominican Friary of Guildford. The Countess of Richmond and mother of King Henry VII often stayed at the Royal Manor in Woking. St John Fisher was her confessor, 1497 – 1509. He is thought to have lived at Fisher's Farm, Old Woking and it is possible that he had a retreat house at the St John's Lye End near the Hermitage. It is said that there was a bargee's beer house there in late Victorian times known as the Fisher's Retreat.

In 1908, St Hugh's Church and Presbytery were built by Father Henry Drage. He was Knaphill's first resident priest. He moved to Walworth in 1912 and was succeeded by Father Stanley Mason. In 1914 Father Mason became an army chaplain attached to Inkerman Barracks, a post he held until 1922 when he was appointed to Sutton Place.

As the congregation grew, St Hugh's church became too small and Mass was celebrated at various venues, among them were Brookwood Hospital, Inkerman Barracks and the British Legion Hall in the Broadway. The present church in Victoria Road was built in 1971.

Listed Buildings

Although the main settlement of Knaphill is now centred on Anchor Hill and the High Street, this area did not really develop until the mid-19th century through the prosperity of the local brickworks. The remnants of the much smaller and older settlement are notably at Lower Knaphill where Anchor Hill joins Barrs Lane.

During the early 19th century this area was known as Whitfield. The area has a strong character with several statutory listed buildings from the 16th and 17th centuries, together with a number of 18th century properties on the 'Local List', all situated in a tight knit group. It comprises of Anchor Hill from the Royal Oak public house through to Littlewick Road eastwards up to Whitfield Court Barn, together with a small section of Robin Hood Road up to Nuthurst. The area is visually important as it marks the entrance into the centre of Knaphill.

Whitfield Court in Littlewick Road is Grade II listed and is still a prominent feature in Knaphill today. It dates from the 16th century, although it was partially rebuilt with extensions in the 18th and 19th centuries. It is a prominent brick building with a timber-framed core and consists of three bays with a large lobby entrance. It was also once the subject of a detailed book by local author Philip Arnold. Its barn is also Grade II listed and goes back to the 18th century.

Barely visible to the casual passer-by these days is Bluegates, also in Littlewick Road, a 16th century timber-framed private residence with late 19th century additions. Its interior consists of a visible timber-framing with substantial ceiling joists and a renovated brick fireplace with wooden lintel. Once part of a much larger expanse of land, Bluegates field is now known as Waterers Park. Bluegates was Grade II listed in October 1973.

Also in Littlewick Road, near the junction with Barrs Lane, is Inwoods, which dates back to the 16th century with an 18th century restoration to its lefthand gable at the front. It is timber-framed with a brick infill and has three bays with cross wings at either end with a lobby entrance. Inwoods has two storeys with an attic in the left gable.

Nuthurst in Robin Hood Road is a late mid-18th century former farmhouse with Flemish bond brick with first-floor tile hanging to rear, gabled old plain tile roofs, and brick stacks, including symmetrical end stacks to front and lateral stacks to rear service wings. The building was Grade II listed in December 1969 and is most noted for its connection with the alleged murder of its lodger, Hilary Rougier, in 1926.

Brookwood Farm House in Robin Hood Road at its junction with Locksley Drive was listed in September 1975 whilst 'still in a dilapidated state'. The farmhouse dates back to the 16th century with extensions recorded as being made in the 19th century.

The Barley Mow Inn, which closed down in 1921, still exists as a private dwelling, now called Barley Mow House, at the junction of Barley Mow Lane and Chobham Road. The old pub dated back to the 17th century and is now a Grade II listed building. Its landlord in 1785 was one Thomas Blackman. It is said that the house was once a royal hunting lodge that was part of Windsor Great Forest. A fireplace in the house bears the coat of arms of Charles I and is the only other known example to exist outside Windsor Castle itself.

An early 1900s view of The Barley Mow pub. (Now Barley Mow House)

The ghost of a headless man, thought to be a soldier killed in a drunken brawl outside the pub, is said to walk in the road with his head tucked under his arm. His head was cut off apparently to prevent his identity from being known. The ghost of a woman dressed in brown has also been seen and it is said that she quickly disappears when approached. Neither of these sightings are recent, though.

Across the road from the former Barley Mow pub is Stillwell Cottage in Chobham Road, which dates back to the 16th-17th century and is timber-framed with brick cladding below and plain tiled above, with a plain tiled roof. Its ground floor windows feature cambered heads. Still quite easy to view from the road, it has a door on the right to the lobby entrance and an under pent roof porch on wooden supports.

Longcroft Cottage in Barrs Lane dates back to the 18th century and is a timber-framed building that has brick cladding. It has a tiled roof with end chimney stacks. It is two storeys with a 'cat slide' type extension that was added to the rear during the mid-20th century.

Some other buildings in Knaphill are listed as 'buildings of architectural significance' and these include: Nursery House in Barrs Lane, Holy Trinity Church in Chobham Road, and The Royal Oak at the foot of Anchor Hill. Other buildings are listed as 'buildings of townscape merit' and these include: Brookwood Farm Cottage in Bagshot Road, Lipscombe Farm in Chobham Road, The Anchor public house in Lower Guildford Road, Haven House in Limecroft Road, Daphne Cottage, and The Robin Hood public house in Robin Hood Road. Also included are No's 31-105 Seymour Court in Raglan Road, Wellington Terrace in Victoria Road (formerly Barrack Road), and No's 67,69,71,73, 75 and 93 in the High Street.

Public Houses

The Anchor, at the junction of High Street and Lower Guildford Road in Knaphill, enjoyed a healthy clientele during the late Victorian era, mainly due to the development around the village and the emergence of other various institutions.

A 1937 coach trip to Bognor Regis organised by the Anchor Pub.

In 1851 the pub was being run by a James Lee aged 42. By 1861 his widow, Sarah, who was now 48, was in charge. They had one son and three daughters. The 1881 census shows that the landlord then was a 34-year-old David Stevens. He and his wife Jane, also 34, had two sons and seven daughters.

The Anchor Hotel, as it was originally known, was the site of the annual 'Whit Fair'. Across the road in Highclere Road was a cricket field where an annual cricket match between teams from the top and bottom of the village was held. The original drayman's store for taking deliveries still exists and is located next to where the New Haweli Express Indian takeaway is now situated in the High Street.

***

The Royal Oak, situated at the bottom of Anchor Hill, is the only survivor of three pubs in 'Lower Knaphill' and dates back to the 17th century. In the mid-19th century, Wesleyan Ministers formed a Sunday school which met there until the completion of the original Methodist church in 1867.

In 1851 the landlord was William Collyer who ran it with his wife, Sarah. By 1891 the pub was being run by Alfred and Phoebe Brighton.

The Royal Oak is not Grade II listed, but is recorded by Woking Borough Council as a 'building of architectural significance'.

The other two pubs in Lower Knaphill were The Royal Standard that was tucked away behind the old village forge. It first appeared on the 1861 census and was being run by James and Ann Meetings. The pub closed down in the 1920s. The other pub, the Queens Head in Robin Hood Road, ceased trading and was demolished in the mid-1980s.

***

Formerly known as The Nags Head until the mid-1980s, The Hunters Lodge in Bagshot Road, which dates back to the 18th century, was a popular watering hole for the navvies and labourers who worked on the construction of the Basingstoke Canal up to its completion in 1794. Later, it became an important social meeting place for those constructing the new London and South Western Railway line, local farm hands, and employees from the nearby Surrey Asylum. In 1881 it was being run by Mark and Sarah Juett.

***

The Robin Hood first appears as a licensed premise in 1861 and, according to that year's census, was being run by Henry Harris. By 1873 the pub appears to have had only a scattering of houses in its immediate vicinity, with the engineer and foreman of the prison living close by in quarters towards Anchor Hill. Between Knaphill and the Woking Prison/Inkerman Barracks site there was a large piece of land called Fulk's Orchard. The Knaphill brickfields were situated on the other side towards Lower Guildford Road and the top of Anchor Hill.

A family record of Albert Jackson, a soldier at the barracks, who later became the first man to drive a public service vehicle in the area, suggests that The Robin Hood was often frequented by warders from the hospital and labourers from the brickfields. The pub now serves the communities of Lower Knaphill, Goldsworth Park, and St John's.

***

The Garibaldi was built towards the end of the 1860s. The 1871 census shows it as being run by Charles and Ann Smith, who had one son. Its beamed structure, although not listed, is a fine example of late 19th century public house design.

Its drayman's delivery store still exists to the side of the pub and can be identified by the high small door at the front of the structure. This is where beer and wine barrels would have been off-loaded from horse-drawn carts. In the late 1990s it was rebranded The Hooden Takes a Knap, but fortunately regained its former identity as The Garibaldi following a further change of ownership in 2005.

***

The Crown in the High Street first appears as a 'beer house' in the 1871 census. Its landlord at the time was William Coombs, aged 56, who ran the premises with his wife Harriett. They had three sons and a daughter. Like many pubs in the area, its two bars are now converted to one following a number of refurbishments since the 1970s.

As recently as 2009, The Crown gained national notoriety when an 'exotic dancer' was cleared of allegedly attacking the lease owner and his wife with a stiletto shoe. Needless to say, the pub is now under new ownership.

War Time 1939-1945

The Hurricane fighter crash in Robin Hood Road: In the early hours of 1 November 1940, a Hurricane fighter plane on a training mission crashed into the roof of a house in Robin Hood Road, Knaphill where a woman was still sleeping.

The pilot, who was already one of the most distinguished pilots of World War II, was Sgt. Laurence Thorogood of RAF 87 Squadron who had bailed out safely and came down in gorse bushes at Horsell. However, the hapless pilot was then met on the ground by Bill Ford, a dairy farmer who erroneously thought that the airman was a member of the Luftwaffe.

Incredibly, the pilot was then escorted to Robin Hood Road where he was re-united with his plane, that was obviously written off in the crash. He was also then able to apologise to the lady who lived at the house for the damage he had caused. Thankfully, she emerged from her cottage unscathed. Laurence Thorogood explained that after flying around trying to find his base, he had to bail out as he ran out of fuel. Later the same day, he reportedly flew a Miles Magister single-engine monoplane trainer with a passenger from Farnborough back to his squadron's main base at Exeter.

Squadron Leader Laurence Arthur Thorogood DFC AE joined RAF 87 Squadron on 14 June 1940 and was thrown straight into the Battle of Britain, destroying a Junkers 88 on 25 August. Commissioned in 1941 he was then posted to India and remained in the Far East until the end of the war. He served with No 9 Squadron Indian Air Force (Hurricane IIc) and 67 Squadron RAF (Spitfire VIII) in the campaign down the Arakan Coast.

Staying in the RAF after the war, he later served in Singapore and Sumatra with 155 Squadron before converting to Vampires on 130 Squadron. After two years instructing on Oxfords at Middle Wallop, he was Adjutant with 615 Squadron, Biggin Hill before moving to Germany in 1951 to fly Vampires with 118 and 94 Squadrons. He served on the Thor missile system before finishing his illustrious career as a civilian in Whitehall.

Sadly, Laurence Thorogood passed away in December 2005.

***

The 1943 Mosquito bomber crash: During a storm on the afternoon of Saturday, 6 November 1943 a Hunsdon (Hertfordshire) based twin-engine DH98 Mosquito from RAF 29 Squadron, Mk XII (Serial no. HK140) was heavily buffeted and began to break up over Brookwood Hospital in Knaphill. The plane spiralled to the ground, close to the gates of the old East Lodge in Lower Guildford Road, killing both crew members.

Brian Jones, who now lives in Australia, was a young boy growing up in Knaphill during the war and remembers the 'big bang' caused by the impact of the wooden framed aircraft hitting the ground as he sheltered with his mother and grandmother in an air raid shelter nearby. On hearing the 'all clear' they raced to the junction of Victoria Road and Lower Guildford Road, only to be told by A.R.P. wardens that it wasn't an air raid, but not to go any further as there was 'complete carnage, live ammunition, flames and dead bodies down there'.

Another Knaphill resident, John Gray, who lived in the Broadway, remembers witnessing the whole drama as a boy from Waterers Park. The plane was flying through a 'dry storm' when it appeared to be hit by a lightning strike. John's brother later went to the crash site and retrieved what John described as being a piece of 'blood splattered wreckage.' On returning home with his 'trophy', his horrified mother ordered him to bury it in their garden, but apparently ended up doing it herself.

The old East Lodge that stood on the edge of the hospital grounds suffered superficial damage. The crash site is very close to where the Cubitt Way children's playground is now situated. East Lodge was demolished in 1994 when the hospital land was sold for redevelopment.

RAF records name the crew as Flight Sergeant (Pilot) Thomas Henry Mullard, aged just 20, (pictured) from Morden, Surrey, and Sergeant (Navigator) Ernest William Knox aged 23 from

Normandy, Surrey. Both airmen are buried at the nearby Brookwood Military Cemetery.

I am very indebted to the late pilot's brother, Peter Mullard, for allowing me to gain access to information from the original RAF Flight Logs of 6 November 1943 and the events that lead to the untimely death of Flight Sergeant Thomas Henry Mullard and the plane's navigator Sergeant Ernest William Knox during what was to be their last training flight.

Official RAF Accident Card: The aircraft broke up in a heavy storm, assumed aircraft out of control in cloud, dived and on breaking cloud, pulled out too violently, aircraft breaking up at once.

Accident Investigation Board (AIB) Conclusions: Loss of control in cloud in very turbulent conditions and aircraft broke up due to loads imposed when recovery attempt made. Both wings, fuselage, and tail unit had disintegrated in mid-air.

Extract from Squadron 29 Operations Record: Operations heard from HK140 when it was in cloud at 10,000 feet after completing a 'Ground Control Interception' (GCI) practice, and indications were that the machine broke up fairly low down as the parts were scattered in a fairly small area with the exception of part of the fuselage that had gone into the ground quite deeply. The Mosquito was one of 6,710 of its type built between 1939 and 1945.

The aircraft's history: HK140 was built as a Mosquito Mk II Night Fighter at De Havilland's in Watford, Hertfordshire in March 1943 and was then sent to contractors to have an improved type of Airborne Interceptor Radar fitted. This meant it would later be re-classified as a MK XII Night Fighter. It was delivered ready for service to RAF 29 Squadron on 21 May 1943.

In September 1943 the squadron moved to RAF Ford in Sussex and pilot Thomas Mullard and his navigator Ernest Knox were posted to the squadron towards the end of October 1943 to be trained for overseas service. The crew were due to be posted to Italy the week after the crash.

A war time view of Anchor Hill, Knaphill after railings had been removed

Dog fights & other skirmishes: Many dogfights occurred in the skies above Knaphill during the war and on one particular occasion the Luftwaffe got the upper hand as an RAF Spitfire was shot down.

The plane crashed at Inkerman Barracks, sadly costing the lives of a number of Canadian soldiers who were stationed there. Fortunately, the pilot had bailed out safely.

Another incident still remembered by some senior local residents is one of a German Bomber that was over Knaphill in broad daylight with RAF fighter planes in hot pursuit. Local children were in their classroom, but could hear the bomber jettisoning its bomb cache nearby.

In their uncertainty, worried mothers and other relatives raced to the school fearing that it had been hit, but were relieved to find it still intact and their children safe. A house was destroyed in Bagshot Road and a number of the jettisoned bombs reportedly fell onto land at Brookwood Cemetery.

An early 1900s view of the junction of the Broadway and the High Street

Crimes and Misdemeanours

The curious case of Hilary Rougier: William Lerwill and his family moved to Nuthurst in Robin Hood Road, Lower Knaphill in June 1926. Lodging with the family was 77-year-old Guernsey-born bachelor and former farmer, Hilary Rougier, who was soon to become a regular patient of the local GP, Dr A.H. Brewer. On 24 August 1926 the doctor was called to an emergency at the house. The doctor found Rougier in a coma and diagnosed that he had suffered a severe cerebral haemorrhage during the night. He died a few hours later of what the doctor at the time recorded as 'natural causes'.

Following the death and funeral, the dead man's family became concerned over the loss of his fortune, in today's terms about £200,000, and concerns of fraud and theft surfaced, particularly when Mr Rougier's bank passbook was found with details of cheques paid out to the Lerwills. In fact, his Last Will and Testament left just £50.

These issues brought about a number of suspicions that Mr Rougier's death was in fact a murder and in March 1928, some eighteen months after his death, the body was exhumed by Surrey Police from the small churchyard at nearby St. John's. Enquiries were made in Knaphill and the surrounding area prior to the exhumation and every witness was pledged to the utmost secrecy. Extraordinary precautions were taken to prevent the identity of the person becoming known. At the time of the exhumation a piece of the local common was even dug up as a distraction from the exhumation work itself.

Following the exhumation, Dr Roche Lynch, Home Office analyst, found *alkaloid morphine* present in the organs. The sample taken indicated that Mr Rougier may have been forced to take a considerable quantity shortly before death.

Dr Lynch said Superintendent Eric Boshier of Surrey Police had handed him one hundred and nineteen articles taken from the Nuthurst residence in Lower Knaphill. A considerable number of these proved to be food preparation essences. He was reserving examination of the articles until it became necessary to do so.

The body was also examined by Sir Bernard Spilsbury who, in 1910, was involved in the famous case of Dr Crippin. Spilsbury rejected the idea that the cause of death was natural, as a high level of morphine had been found in the body. During his illustrious career Spilsbury also performed thousands of autopsies, not only for murder victims, but also of executed criminals. A detailed enquiry lasting months and a lengthy inquest failed to lead to any criminal charges against the Lerwill family or anyone else. It remains that Mr Rougier's considerable fortune had been dissipated.

His 'friends', the Lerwill family, later appeared to rise from apparent debt to a sudden state of affluence, but there was no evidence of any criminal offences and they were never charged. So, did the Lerwill's get away with murder?

Well, there is a modern saying that goes, *'What goes around comes around',* and this is so very true so far as William Lerwill was concerned....

There was no point in Mr. Rougier's relatives pursuing the Lerwills for his money as it had clearly been spent and could not be returned, even if litigation was finally successful. As for the big house in Lower Knaphill, the Lerwills decamped having paid only a third of the rent they owed its rightful owner.

William Lerwill, a man always with an eye for the main chance, later sued two newspapers for libel, successfully bringing him the best part of £5,000. He then deserted his wife and children and went to live in Canada. By 1933 he was back in England, virtually broke and leaving one cheque after another bouncing behind him.

One day in March 1934, he was walking down a street in Coombe Martin in Devon when a policeman stopped him and challenged him about an unpaid hotel bill. Whatever his failings, Lerwill was never guilty of indecision. He promptly produced a small bottle of prussic acid, swallowed the contents, and fell dead at the officer's feet. So, was this the suicide of a man tired of running? Or, was it indeed a bizarre murder confession?

It is important to note that William Lerwill was legally cleared of the murder and also later succeeded with a libel action against the press. A possible, if not probable, conclusion is that Hilary Rougier, for reasons unknown, may have wished to kill himself.

***

Flora Derigo: Surrey Constabulary records show that on 22 December 1924 two men heard screams coming from the Basingstoke Canal near St John's. They found a woman clinging to a lock gate and pulled her clear. She immediately indicated that she had thrown her baby into the water in a fit of temper. A doctor and the police were called and the canal was dredged. The woman, Flora Derigo, was arrested and held at Knaphill Police Station.

Flora's husband was an American soldier who had returned to the USA, and although he had made all the arrangements for her to join him, her family had prevented the reunion. She was now living with a Sidney Smith and six weeks before his death, her baby, Clifton Barrington Martin Derigo, was born. Smith fell out with Flora and moved away on 18 December and the culmination of all the problems in her life resulted in the baby being thrown into the canal.

During an inquest in January 1925, Flora was committed for trial on a charge of wilful murder. Flora later appeared on 25 March at Surrey Assizes where she pleaded guilty to infanticide. This was accepted by the court and Flora was bound over in the sum of £50.

***

Alec Storey (Lawrence): On 11 February 1958, Alec Storey (17) turned up on his motor bike at Knaphill Police Station in Oak Tree Road spur and pulled a .22 pistol from his waist and said that he had shot his foster mother five times in the head.

Originally known as Alec Taylor Lawrence before being adopted, he stated that he had borrowed the gun from a neighbour for target practice. He said that he had accidentally discharged the gun and his mother came to the bedroom to inspect the damage.

Alec Storey wrote in his statement to police that, 'She then got down on the floor to look at the bullet hole in the carpet. While she was like that I pulled the trigger which resulted in her being hit on the head. I think she jerked forward straight away and fell flat on her tummy, with her head on its left side. I then aimed a second shot at her and emptied the magazine in her head.'

Police went to the four-hundred-year-old converted farmhouse on Pirbright Green and found the murdered woman. The juvenile was eventually charged and appeared at the Old Bailey in London. He was expensively educated, but was described in court as an extremely disturbed young man who had been dug from a bombed building in London when very small and given over to adoption by a family struggling to make their way. He felt he did not belong to anybody or anywhere.

Evidence was given by Detective Sergeant Henry Helsdon. Storey was found guilty of manslaughter on the grounds of diminished responsibility and was sentenced to three years.

The former police station in Knaphill still exists, but has been converted into a private residence.

***

Diane Holliday: According to an article in *The Observer* on Sunday, 8 February 1998, Dodi Fayed had a secret lovechild. The child's mother, Ms Diane Holliday, claimed that Dodi's daughter, Marni, was nine months old when Mr Fayed died in the Paris car crash alongside Diana, Princess of Wales. Diane Holliday, who was 36 at the time, was a British hotel consultant from Victoria Road, Knaphill.

Marni, whose photograph is said to bear a striking resemblance to Mr Fayed, was born in an American hospital in November 1996, according to her mother.

Ms Holliday initially handed her baby over for adoption in the United States, but then hired a London lawyer, whose clients have included the Duchess of York and Sarah Brightman, in an attempt to win her return.

Her solicitor, Douglas Alexiou, said in a statement to *The Observer:* 'I am instructed by my client to confirm that she is the mother of the child. I have the birth certificate in front of me and the father is the late Dodi Fayed. I am satisfied that the instructions are correct.'

The battle over Marni had become the latest chapter in the long-running feud between Mohammed al-Fayed, Dodi's father, and his bitter rival, Tiny Rowland. Scotland Yard investigated allegations arising from the claim.

Dodi was Mohammed al-Fayed's eldest son, so his daughter – if paternity was proved – could be an apparent heir to the Harrods fortune. Ms Holliday claimed that she had a series of meetings with Dodi's father at which he expressed an interest in bringing the child back to Britain, but that she had fallen out with him.

Mr Rowland told *The Observer*: 'She told me a long story about Dodi and how he was the father of her baby who was born on 20 November 1996, in America. She said Dodi asked her to have an abortion. The baby was adopted.'

Mr Rowland said he believed there was DNA evidence to prove Dodi was the father. There was then a dispute between Ms Holliday and Mr Rowland, who had made a complaint to the police.

A Scotland Yard spokesman confirmed that police had carried out an investigation into an alleged financial deception.

Ms Holliday denied any wrongdoing. Friends of Ms Holliday, who also had two teenage children, said she met Dodi at the Ritz Hotel in Paris in 1995. At the time, she was separated from her husband pending a divorce. In the next five months, there were frequent meetings at Dodi's Paris and Mayfair apartments and her former home in Bracknell, Berkshire.

In July 1996 she discovered that she was five months pregnant and broke the news to Dodi. Her friends denied Dodi wanted an abortion at first, but said at the time that he went along with her wish for one. However, Ms Holliday later decided not to go through with it. Without telling Dodi, she travelled to the United States, where an agency arranged an adoption.

Diane Holliday again hit the headlines in 2009 after Erkin Guney, the owner of Brookwood Cemetery, was comprehensively cleared by a jury of soliciting her murder. The case was to prove that Erkin Guney had become the victim of one of the UK's biggest-ever miscarriages of justice.

In April 2009, Erkin Guney went on trial for soliciting the murder of his late father's lover, Diane Holliday. Erkin was accused of hiring a hitman to kill her to prevent her from benefiting from his father, Ramadan Guney's, estate. Ms Holliday was to be involved in a serious, in fact fatal, car accident – or so it seemed.

Erkin was one of six children of Ramadan and his wife Suyehla Guney. Suyehla died in 1992. Ramadan, the millionaire owner of Brookwood Cemetery, later had a child with Diane Holliday.

The hitman allegedly hired by Erkin was actually an undercover police officer. Holliday's supposed car crash was a ruse allegedly concocted by the police. She was not actually involved in an accident. Erkin's defence was that he knew all along about the undercover plot and was playing along with it. He was sensationally acquitted in May 2009.

There had also been suspicions of foul play concerning Ramadan, whose death in 2006 at the age of 74 was attributed at the time to a heart attack. His body was later exhumed, but no charges were ever brought.

Even today, the saga continues.

***

Daniel Gonzalez: A schizophrenic serial killer from Knaphill who murdered four people in a number of attacks throughout 2004 was 26-year-old Daniel Gonzalez. The murders had sent shock waves around the whole country.

His victims, all chosen at random, were: retired doctor Derek Robinson, 76, and his wife, Jean, 68, from Highgate, North London; Kevin Molloy, 46, who was killed in Tottenham, North London; and Marie Harding, 73, who was murdered near Worthing in Sussex. Two men survived his attacks: Peter King, 61, who was attacked in Portsmouth, Hampshire; and Koumis Constantinou, 59, who was knifed in North London.

Two days before the first murder, Gonzalez gave himself two black eyes by punching himself in the face, and proceeded to run naked through the streets of Knaphill in front of schoolchildren and their parents, before running back to his home in Southwood Avenue.

A 2009 report into his mental health care revealed that although he attended nearly 60 appointments with doctors and psychiatrists, more could have been done by the NHS to prevent the tragedies. Gonzalez had been found dead in his Broadmoor cell in August 2007 after slashing his wrists with the shards of plastic from broken compact discs.

Knaphill and the War of the Worlds

Too close for comfort? Whilst neighbouring Horsell enjoys its association with the famous fictional H.G. Wells novel of 1898, Knaphill does actually get a mention!

'And far away towards Knaphill I saw the flashes of trees and hedges and wooden buildings suddenly set alight.' – H.G. Wells

The novel has since been transferred to the big screen and was also adapted by Jeff Wayne in the 1970s into a musical format. The musical version has since been reborn and Jeff Wayne has enjoyed a number of successful world tours with his illustrious show since 2006.

Rare early 1900s view of the Broadway looking towards Knaphill Village

Knaphill Football Club

Knaphill Football Club began its life in 1924 at Waterers Park. Waterers Park was left to Woking Urban District Council in 1924 by Anthony Waterer of Knaphill Nursery. The Recreation Ground was originally part of the nursery and was formerly known as Bluegates Field. The current park was landscaped by Woking Council between 1924 and 1928.

In 2005 Knaphill F.C. moved to their current ground in Redding Way and gained senior status in 2007 after winning the Surrey Intermediate League Championship.

In August 2011 the club played their part in national football history when they became the first team from the mainland to play a competitive league match at any level against a team from the Channel Islands, when they travelled to an away fixture at newly formed Guernsey F.C. in the Combined Counties League Division One.

Knaphill's other football club is Knaphill Athletic F.C., who were formed as recently as 2010 by the former committee and members of Surrey Athletic and Knaphill F.C. 'A' & 'B' teams. The club was created to provide participation football at all levels throughout the intermediate and junior levels of adult football.

Based at Waterers Park, the club's first season in 2010-11 saw three sides compete in the Guildford & Woking Alliance League, with the new football club making an instant impact. The club now competes in the Surrey Intermediate League.

The Village Identity and its Future

The sale of most of Knaphill Common in the early 1860s by The London Necropolis and Mausoleum Company and the naming of the new Woking Invalid and Woking Women's prisons are perhaps the earliest signs that Knaphill's village identity, and clearly its name, was being overlooked by local authorities and developers as the nearby community of Woking grew more in stature as a town.

Since the railway arrived in 1838, Brookwood slowly became more of a village in its own right as further growth continued along Connaught Road. Indeed, the renaming of the Surrey County Asylum to Brookwood Hospital in 1919 is probably the main reason why confusion exists over various parts of the real Knaphill boundary today.

When work began on the Goldsworth Park housing estate in the 1970s, further encroachment into Knaphill occurred as parts of Lower Knaphill, around what is now Lockfield Drive and Creston Avenue, was redeveloped.

The recent re-working of political boundaries for election purposes by Woking Borough Council also hasn't helped as we see Knaphill's historical border becoming even fuzzier. Indeed, Surrey Police, Surrey County Council, Woking Borough Council, and the Post Office all have very different ideas from each other as to where Knaphill actually starts and ends.

As Woking Borough Council begins its controversial sale of Knaphill's Brookwood Farm, which is located just off

Sparvell Road, it's evident that many people, including potential housing developers, erroneously believe that the farmland is part of Brookwood. Indeed, this is a constant misconception by many of the village's newer incumbents and by some in the local press.

Importantly though, Knaphill, whilst not archetypal as in picturesque, is still rich in its own history. Its contribution to the whole of Woking Borough and to parts of Surrey Heath, particularly as an area for steady and meaningful employment down the years, has been well documented.

Decisions by local government however, will continue to determine its future. It remains to be seen what this future holds, but there are already concerns that any further redevelopment of the village will need to have a revised infrastructure, and that in itself will bring about a number of further changes to the very fabric of this historical place that some people still struggle to call Knaphill.

www.theknaphillian.com